Introduction

Congratulations, you have found the most comprehensive and streamlined RHCSA study guide available. This book only contains the 111 question sample RHCSA exam (EX200).

Red Hat Enterprise Linux licenses are expensive, therefore it is recommended to download a free copy of CentOS or Scientific Linux because they are the most like Red Hat Enterprise Linux.

QUESTION 1
Configure a cron task.
User natasha must configure a cron job, local time 14:23 runs and executes: */bin/echo hiya every day.

Correct Answer/Explanation:
crontab -e -u natasha 23 14 /bin/echo hiya
crontab -l -u natasha
systemctl enable crond
systemctl restart crond

QUESTION 2
SELinux must run in enforcing mode.

Correct Answer/Explanation:
# vi /etc/sysconfig/selinux
SELINUX=enforcing

QUESTION 3
Create the user named eric and deny to interactive login.

Correct Answer/Explanation:
useradd eric
passwd eric
vi /etc/passwd
eric:x:499:499::/home/eric:/sbin/nologin

The shell or program that should start at login time is specified in the /etc/passwd file. By default, RedHat Enterprise Linux assigns the /bin/bash shell to users. To deny the interactive login, you should write /sbin/nologin or /bin/false instead of the default login shell /bin/bash.

QUESTION 4
There are two different networks 192.168.0.0/24 and 192.168.1.0/24. Where 192.168.0.254 and 192.168.1.254 static IP addresses are assigned to servers. Configure networking with a static IP address for the server on the 192.168.0.0/24 network.   Verify your network settings by pinging 192.168.0.0/24 network's host.

Correct Answer/Explanation:
# vi /etc/sysconfig/network
NETWORKING=yes
HOSTNAME=servername.example.com
GATEWAY=192.168.0.1
# service network restart
# vi /etc/sysconfig/network-scripts/ifcfg-eth0
DEVICE=eth0
ONBOOT=yes
BOOTPROTO=static
IPADDR=192.168.0.254
NETMASK=255.255.255.0

```
GATEWAY=192.168.0.1
# ifdown eth0
# ifup eth0
# ping 192.168.0.254
```

QUESTION 5

Install a FTP server, and request an anonymous download from the /var/ftp/pub catalog. Note that it needs you to configure yum direct yum to the already existing file server.

Correct Answer/Explanation:

```
# cd /etc/yum.repos.d
# vim local.repo
[local]
name=local.repo
baseurl=file:///mnt
enabled=1
gpgcheck=0
# yum makecache
# yum install -y vsftpd
# service vsftpd restart
# chkconfig vsftpd on
# chkconfig --list vsftpd
# vim /etc/vsftpd/vsftpd.conf
anonymous_enable=YES
```

QUESTION 6

Create a 512M partition, make it as ext4 file system, mounted automatically under /mnt/data and which takes effect automatically at boot.

Correct Answer/Explanation:

```
# fdisk /dev/vda
n        ( for new partition )
l        ( for logical partitions )
Enter    ( for starting Cylinder)
+512M ( for finishing Cylinder)
p        ( p to verify the partitions lists and remember the partition's name for below )
w        ( to write on partitions table )
# partprobe /dev/vda
# mkfs  -t ext4 /dev/vda5
# mkdir  -p /data
# vim /etc/fstab
/dev/vda5 /data  ext4 defaults 0 0
# mount -a
```

QUESTION 7

Set cronjob for user natasha to do /bin/echo hiya at 14:23.

Correct Answer/Explanation:

```
# crontab -e -u natasha
23 14 * * * /bin/echo hiya
wq!
```

QUESTION 8
Configure the FTP service in your system, allow remote access to anonymous login and download the program by this service. Configure the service so that it runs after rebooting.

Correct Answer/Explanation:
```
yum install vsftpd
/etc/init.d/vsftpd start
chkconfig vsftpd on
```

QUESTION 9
A package named zsh is dumped on ftp://server1.example.com under /pub/updates and your FTP server is 192.168.0.254. Install the package zsh.

Correct Answer/Explanation:
```
# rpm -ivh ftp://server1.example.com/pub/updates/zsh-*
```
or
Login to the ftp server using the anonymous user:
```
# ftp ftp://server1.example.com
```

```
# cd pub
# cd updates
# mget zsh-* ( Download the package zsh )
```
Quit from the ftp prompt: bye
```
# rpm -ivh zsh-* (Install the package zsh )
```

Verify package is installed:
```
# rpm -q zsh
```

QUESTION 10
Configure the verification mode of your host account and password as LDAP, and that it can login successfully through ldapuser30. The password is set as "password".
The certificate can be downloaded from http://ip/dir/ldap.crt. After the user logs on the user has no host directory unless you configure the autofs – See the following questions for configuring autofs.

Correct Answer/Explanation:
```
system-config-authentication
```
LDAP Server: ldap//instructor.example.com (In fully qualified domain form) OR
```
# yum groupinstall directory-client
```
Kerberos packages may be installed by default, but make sure that the appropriate packages are installed for the Kerberos client: krb5-workstation, pam-krb5, sssd
https://access.redhat.com/documentation/en-us/red_hat_enterprise_linux/6/html/managing_smart_cards/installing-kerberos

```
# system-config-authentication
```

User Account Database: LDAP
LDAP Search Base DN: dc=example,dc=com
LDAP Server: ldap://instructor.example.com (In fully qualified domain form)
Download CA Certificate
Authentication Method: LDAP password
getent passwd ldapuser30 (Verify)

QUESTION 11

Your System is going to use as a Router for two networks. One network is 192.168.0.0/24 and the other network is 192.168.1.0/24. Both networks' IP address have been assigned. How will you forward the packets from one network to the other network?

Correct Answer/Explanation:
# echo "1" >/proc/sys/net/ipv4/ip_forward
# vi /etc/sysctl.conf
net.ipv4.ip_forward = 1

If you want to enable communication between different networks, you have to enable IP forwarding. To enable routing during a running session just set /proc/sys/net/ipv4/ip_forward to 1. The /etc/sysctl.conf file setting will automatically turn on the IP forwarding features on next boot.

QUESTION 12

Configure your Host Name, IP Address, Gateway and DNS as follows:
Host name: workstation.domain30.example.com
/etc/sysconfig/network
hostname=abc.com
IP Address: 172.24.30.30/24
Gateway: 172.24.30.1
DNS: 172.24.30.1

Correct Answer/Explanation:
# cd /etc/sysconfig/network-scripts/
# ls
# vim ifcfg-eth0
IPADDR=172.24.30.30
GATEWAY=172.24.30.1
DNS1=172.24.30.1
# vim /etc/sysconfig/network
HOSTNAME=workstation.domain30.example.com

OR configure using the graphical interface:
System->Preference->Network Connections (Configure IP Address, Gateway and DNS)
# vim /etc/sysconfig/network (Configure Host Name)
HOSTNAME=workstation.domain30.example.com

QUESTION 13

We are working on /data with initially the size being 2GB. The /dev/test0/lvtestvolume is mounted on /data. Now you require more space on /data but you already added all disks belong to physical volume. You found that you have 5GB of unallocated space on the same hard drive, /dev/test0. Increase the size of volume lvtestvolume by 5GB.

Correct Answer/Explanation:
fdisk /dev/hda
n   (for new partition)
l   (for logical partition)
Enter   (for the starting cylinder)
+100M (for the final cylinder)
p   (p to verify the partitions lists and remember the partition's name for below)
t   (to change the System ID of partition)
8e   (8e means LVM type partition)
w   (to write on partitions table)
partprobe (or reboot)
pvcreate /dev/hda6 (let's suppose the partition number just created was hda6).
vgextend test0 /dev/hda6 (the vgextend command adds the physical disk to the volume group)
lvextend -L +5120M /dev/test0/lvtestvolume
lvdisplay /dev/test0/lvtestvolume (Verify)

QUESTION 14
Configure autofs to make sure after login, it has the home directory autofs, which is shared as /rhome/ldapuser30 at the ip: 172.24.30.10, and it also requires that other LDAP users can use the home directory normally.

Correct Answer/Explanation:
chkconfig autofs on
cd /etc/
vim /etc/auto.master
/rhome /etc/auto.ldap
cp auto.misc auto.ldap
vim auto.ladp
ldapuser30 -rw,soft,intr 172.24.30.10:/rhome/ldapuser30
* -rw,soft,intr 172.16.30.10:/rhome/&
# service autofs stop
# server autofs start
# showmount -e 172.24.30.10
# su - ladpuser30

QUESTION 15
User mary must configure a task to run at the local time at 14:23 every day, echo "Hello World.".

Correct Answer/Explanation:
crontab -u mary -e 23 14   * * * echo "Hello World."

QUESTION 16

A yum repository has been provided at http::/server.domain11.example.com/pub/x86_64/Server. Configure your system to use this location as a default repository.

Correct Answer/Explanation:
vim/etc/yum.repos/base.repo
[base]
name=base
baseurl=http://server.domain11.example.com/pub/x86_64/Server
gpgcheck=0
enable=1
Save and Exit
Use the command yum list for validation. If the yum configuration is not correct then it will not be possible to answer the following yum related questions.

QUESTION 17

Download the document from ftp://instructor.example.com/pub/testfile, find all lines containing [abcde] and redirect to the /mnt/answer document, then rearrange the order according the original content.

Correct Answer/Explanation:
Download the file to /tmp:
grep [abcde] /tmp/testfile > /mnt/answer

QUESTION 18

Whoever creates the files/directories on a data group owner should automatically be in the same group owner as data.

Correct Answer/Explanation:
chmod g+s /data
ls -ld /data (Verify)
Permission should be like this: drwxrws--- 2 root sysadmin 4096 Feb 22 17:00 /data
If SGID is set on directory then whichever user creates the files within the directory, the group owner is automatically the owner of file (or directory). To set the SGID: chmod g+s directory. To remove the SGID: chmod g-s directory

QUESTION 19

Create a 2G swap partition which takes effect automatically at boot, and it should not affect the original swap partition.

Correct Answer/Explanation.:
fdisk /dev/sda
p   (checks partitions table)
n   (for new partition)
l   (for logical partition)
Enter   (for the starting cylinder)
+2G   (for the final cylinder)
t   (to change the System ID of partition)

82   (82 means Linux Swap)
p   (p to verify the partitions lists and remember the partition's name for below)
w   (to write on partitions table)
partx -a /dev/sda
partprobe (or reboot)
mkswap /dev/sda8
Record a copy of the UUID shown, or copy it to the clipboard, it will be used in the XXXXXXXXXX within the /etc/fstab file below.
# swapon -a
# vim /etc/fstab
UUID=XXXXXXXXX swap swap defaults 0 0
# swapon -s

QUESTION 20
Change the logical volume capacity named lv2 from 190M to 300M, and the size of the floating range should set between 280 and 320. (This logical volume has been mounted in advance.)

Correct Answer/Explanation:
vgdisplay
(Check the capacity of vg, if the capacity is not enough, need to create pv, vgextend , lvextend)
lvdisplay (Check the lv)
lvextend -L +110M /dev/vg2/lv2
resize2fs /dev/vg2/lv2
mount -a (Verify)

Decrease lvm:
umount /media
fsck -f /dev/vg2/lv2
resize2fs -f /dev/vg2/lv2 100M
lvreduce -L 100M /dev/vg2/lv2
mount -a
lvdisplay (Verify)
OR
e2fsck -f /dev/vg1/lvm02
resize2fs -f /dev/vg1/lvm02
mount /dev/vg1/lvm01 /mnt
lvreduce -L 1G -n /dev/vg1/lvm02
lvdisplay (Verify)

QUESTION 21
You're a system administrator. Using log files is an easy way to monitor the system. Now there are 50 servers running as Mail, Web, Proxy, DNS services, etc. You want to centralize the logs from all servers onto one log server. How will you configure the log server to accept logs from remote hosts?

Correct Answer/Explanation:
By default, the system accepts only the logs generated from local host. To accept logs from other hosts configure the following:
vi /etc/sysconfig/syslog

SYSLOGD_OPTIONS="-m 0 -r"
# service syslog restart

-m 0 disables 'MARK' messages.
-r enables logging from remote machines
-x disables DNS lookups on messages received with -r

QUESTION 22
Create a backup file named /root/backup.tar.bz2, which contains the contents of /usr/local. It must use bzip2 compression.

Correct Answer/Explanation:
cd /usr/local
tar -jcvf /root/backup.tar.bz2
mkdir /test
tar -jxvf /root/backup.tar.bz2 -C /test/

QUESTION 23
Configure a default software repository for your system.
Yum has already been provided to configure your system on
http://server.domain11.example.com/pub/x86_64/Server

Correct Answer/Explanation:
# yum-config-manager --add-repo=http://content.example.com/rhel7.0/x86-64/dvd
# vim content.example.com_rhel7.0_x86_64_dvd.repo
gpgcheck=0
# yumcleanall
# yumrepolist
Almost 4305 packages are in the correct RHEL 7 repository from the DVD.
Configuring yum incorrectly will lead the inability to solve some of following yum related questions.

QUESTION 24
Successfully resolve to server1.example.com where your DNS server is 172.24.254.254.

Correct Answer/Explanation:
vi /etc/resolv.conf
nameserver 172.24.254.254
host server1.example.com

In all Linux clients, the DNS server is specified in /etc/resolv.conf by the nameserver line.

QUESTION 25
The following are requirements to create a user, a user group and the user group's members:
-A group named admin.
-A user named mary, and belonging to admin as the secondary (supplemental) group.
-A user named alice, and belonging to admin as the secondary (supplemental) group.
-A user named bobby, and bobby's login shell should be non-interactive. Bobby does not belong to admin as the secondary (supplemental) group.

Mary, alice, and bobby must have their password set to be "password"

Correct Answer/Explanation:
groupadd admin
useradd -G admin mary
useradd -G admin alice
useradd -s /sbin/nologin bobby
echo "password" | passwd --stdin mary
echo "password" | passwd --stdin alice
echo "password" | passwd --stdin bobby

QUESTION 26
Find all lines in the file /usr/share/dict/words that contain the string seismic. Put a copy of all these lines in their original order in the file /root/wordlist. /root/wordlist should contain no empty lines and all lines must be exact copies of the original lines in /usr/share/dict/words.

Correct Answer/Explanation:
grep seismic /usr/share/dict/words > /root/wordlist

QUESTION 27
Configure a HTTP server, which can be accessed through http://station.domain30.example.com.

Please download the released page from http://ip/dir/example.html

Correct Answer/Explanation:
yum install -y httpd
chkconfig httpd on
cd /var/www/html
wget http://ip/dir/example.html
cp example.com index.html
vim /etc/httpd/conf/httpd.conf
NameVirtualHost 192.168.0.254:80
<VirtualHost 192.168.0.254:80>
DocumentRoot /var/www/html/
ServerName station.domain30.example.com
</VirtualHost>

QUESTION 28
Configure NTP.
Configure NTP service, & synchronize the server time using NTP server: classroom.example.com

Correct Answer/Explanation:
Configure the Client:
yum -y install chrony
vim /etc/chrony.conf
server classroom.example.com iburst
systemctl enable chronyd
systemctl restart chronyd

timedatectl status (Verify)

QUESTION 29
Configure your NFS services. Share the directory by the NFS Shared services.

Correct Answer/Explanation:
/etc/init.d/rpcbind start
/etc/init.d/nfslock start
/etc/init.d/nfs start
chkconfig rpcbind on
chkconfig nfslock on
chkconfig nfs on
showmount -e localhost

QUESTION 30
Configure your host name, IP address, gateway and DNS with the following.
Host name: dtop5.dn.ws.com
IP Address: 172.28.10.5/4
Gateway: 172.28.10.1
DNS: 172.28.10.1

Correct Answer/Explanation:
# vim /etc/sysconfig/network
NETWORKING=yes
HOSTNAME=dtop5.dn.ws.com
GATEWAY=172.28.10.1
Configure IP address, gateway and DNS configuration with Network Manager:

Check these two options:

- Connect automatically
- Available to all users

Click "Apply", save and exit, and then restart your network service:

service network restart

Check gateway:
#vim /etc/sysconfig/network
NETWORKING=yes
HOSTNAME=dtop5.dn.ws.com
GATEWAY=172.28.10.1
Check Host Name:
vim /etc/hosts

```
172.28.10.5      dtop5.dn.ws.com dtop5   # Added  by NetworkManager
127.0.0.1        localhost.localdomain    localhost
::1              dtop.dn.ws.com  dtop5  localbost5.localdomain5 localhost5
```

Check DNS:
vim /etc/resolv.conf
Generated by NetworkManager
Search dn.ws.com
Nameserver 172.28.10.1
Check Gateway:
vim /etc/sysconfig/network-scripts/ifcfg-eth0

```
DEVICE="eth0"
NM_CONTROLLED="yes"
ONBOOT=yes
TYPE =Ethernet
BOOTPROTO=none
IPADDR 172.28.10.5
PREFIX=24
GATEWAY=172.28.10.1
DNS1=172.28.10.1
DOMAIN=dn.ws.com
DEFROUTE=yes
IPV4_FAILURE_FATAL=yes
IPV6INIT=no
NAME="System eth0"
UUID=3ed110db9-1ad4-8aae-87dd-efd1433d33aa
HWADDR=00:1A:DE:9A:DE:A1
```

QUESTION 31
Add an additional swap partition of 754MB to your system.
The swap partition should automatically mount when your system boots.
Do not remove or otherwise alter any existing swap partitions on your system.

Correct Answer/Explanation:

```
# fdisk -l
# fdisk -cu /dev/vda
p          ( to check partitions )
n          ( for new partition)
l          ( for logical partition)
Enter    ( for the starting cylinder)
+754M ( for the final cylinder)
t          ( to change the System ID of partition )
82        ( 82 means Linux Swap )
p          ( p to verify the partitions lists and remember the partition's name for below )
w          ( to write on partitions table )
# partprobe ( or reboot )
# mkswap /dev/vda5
# vim /etc/fstab
/dev/vda5 swap swap defaults 0 0
wq
# mount -a
# swapon -a
# swapon -s
```

QUESTION 32
Find the files owned by harry, and copy it to this catalog: /opt/dir

Correct Answer/Explanation:
```
# cd /opt/
# mkdir dir
# find / -user harry -exec cp -rfp {} /opt/dir/ \;
```

QUESTION 33
Configure autofs to automatically mount the home directory of LDAP, as required:
server.domain11.example.com use NFS to share the home to your system.
This NFS file system contains a pre-configured home directory of user ldapuserX.
Home directory of ldapuserX is:
server.domain11.example.com /home/guests/ldapuser
Home directory of ldapuserX should automatically mounted to the ldapuserX of the local /home/guests.
Home directory's write permissions must be available for users.
ldapuser1's password is password

Correct Answer/Explanation:
```
# yum install -y autofs
# mkdir /home/rehome
# vim /etc/auto.master
/home/rehome /etc/auto.ldap
# cp /etc/auto.misc /etc/auto.ldap
# vim /etc/auto.ldap
ldapuserX  -fstype=nfs.rw server.domain11.example.com:/home/guests/
# systemctl start autofs
# systemctl enable autofs
```

su - ldapuserX// test

If the above solutions fails to create files or the command prompt is -bash-4.2$, a multi-level directory may exist; In that case change the server.domain11.exarnple.com:/home/guests/ to server.domain11.example.com:/home/guests/ldapuserX. This directory is the real directory.

QUESTION 34
Find the rows that contain abcde from file /etc/testfile, and write it to the file /tmp/testfile, and the sequence is to be the same as the original sequence in /etc/testfile.

Correct Answer/Explanation:

```
# cat /etc/testfile | while read line;
do
echo $line | grep abcde | tee -a /tmp/testfile
done
OR
grep 'abcde' /etc/testfile > /tmp/testfile
```

QUESTION 35
Create a new logical volume.
Name the logical volume as database, belongs to datastore of the volume group, size is 50 PE.
Expansion size of each volume in volume group datastore is 16MB.
Use ext3 to format this new logical volume, this logical volume should automatically mount to /mnt/database

Correct Answer/Explanation:
```
# fdisk -cu /dev/vda    (Creates a 1G partition, modified when needed)
# partx -a /dev/vda
# pvcreate /dev/vdax
# vgcreate datastore /dev/vdax -s 16M
# lvcreate -l 50 -n database datastore
# mkfs.ext3 /dev/datastore/database
# mkdir /mnt/database
# mount /dev/datastore/database /mnt/database/ df -Th
# vi /etc/fstab
/dev/datastore /database /mnt/database/ ext3 defaults 0 0
# mount -a
```

QUESTION 36
Configure /var/tmp/fstab permissions.
Copy the file /etc/fstab to /var/tmp/fstab. Configure /var/tmp/fstab permissions as followings:
Owner of the file /var/tmp/fstab is Root, belongs to group root
File /var/tmp/fstab cannot be executed by any user
User natasha can read and write /var/tmp/fstab
User harry cannot read and write /var/tmp/fstab
All other users {present and future) can read /var/tmp/fstab.

Correct Answer/Explanation:
cp /etc/fstab /var/tmp/
view the owner for /var/tmp/fstab:
setfacl -m u:natasha:rw- /var/tmp/fstab setfacl -m u:harry:--- /var/tmp/fstab
view permissions:
getfacl /var/tmp/fstab

QUESTION 37
Configure the system date & time.

Correct Answer/Explanation:
Graphical Interfaces:
System-->Administration->Date & Time
OR
system-config-date

QUESTION 38
User authentication has been provided by an LDAP domain at 192.168 0.254. Use the following requirements to get ldapuser from that LDAP.
-LdapuserX must be able to login your system, X is your hostname number. But the ldapuser's home directory cannot be mounted, until you realize it is automatically mounted by the autofs server.
-All LDAP user passwords is set to "password".

Correct Answer/Explanation:
system-config-authentication &

QUESTION 39

Configure iptables, there are two domains in the network, the address of the local domain is 172.24.0.0/16, and the other domain is 172.25.0.0/16, & refuse domain is 172.25.0.0/16 to access the server.

Correct Answer/Explanation:
iptables -F
service iptables save
iptables -A INPUT -s 172.25.0.0/16 -j REJECT
service iptables save
service iptables restart

QUESTION 40

Adjust the size of the Logical Volume.

Adjust the size of the Logical Volume, lvo, its file system size should be 290M. Make sure that the contents of this system is complete.

The partition size is rarely accurately created to the same size as required. Therefore, the range 270M to 320M is acceptable.

Correct Answer/Explanation:
Addition steps:
df -hT
lvextend -L +100M /dev/vg0/lvo
lvscan
xfs_growfs /home/ (/home is the mounted directory of the LVM, this step just need to do in the practice environment, and test EXT4 does not need this step.)
resize2fs /dev/vg0/lvo (Use this command to update in the actual exam.)
df -hT
OR
Subtraction steps:
e2fsck -f /dev/vg0/lvo
umount /home
resize2fs /devfvg0/vo/lvo (The final required partition capacity is 100M.)
lvreduce -l 100M /dev/vg0/lvo
mount /dev/vg0/lvo/home
df -hT

QUESTION 41

Configure web services, download from http://instructor.example.com/pub/serverX.html
The services must be still be running after system reboot.

Correct Answer/Explanation:
cd /var/www/html
wget http://instructor.example.com/pub/serverX.html
mv serverX .html index.html
/etc/initd/httpd restart
chkconfig httpd on

QUESTION 42
Create a volume group with 8M extends. Divided a volume group containing 50 extends on
volume group lv (lvshare), make it as ext4 file system, and mounted automatically under /mnt/data/
And the size of the floating range should set between 380M and 400M.

Correct Answer/Explanation:
```
# fdisk
# partprobe ( or reboot )
# pvcreate /dev/vda6
# vgcreate -s 8M vg1 /dev/vda6 -s
# lvcreate -n lvshare -l 50 vg1 -l
# mkfs.ext4 /dev/vg1/lvshare
# mkdir -p /mnt/data
# vim /etc/fstab
/dev/vg1/lvshare /mnt/data ext4 defaults 0 0
# mount -a
# df -h
```

QUESTION 43
Open the ip_forward, and make it take effect permanently.

Correct Answer/Explanation:
```
# vim /etc/sysctl.conf net.ipv4.ip_forward = 1
# sysctl -w (takes effect immediately)
If no "sysctl.conf" option, use these commands:
# sysctl -a | grep net.ipv4
# sysctl -P net.ipv4.ip_forward = 1
# sysctl -w
```

QUESTION 44
Create a new logical volume according to the following requirements:
The logical volume is named database and belongs to the datastore volume group and has a size of 50
extents.
Logical volumes in the datastore volume group should have an extent size of 16 MB.
Format the new logical volume with an ext3 filesystem.
The logical volume should be automatically mounted under /mnt/database at system boot time.

Correct Answer/Explanation:
```
# fdisk -cu /dev/vda
# partx -a /dev/vda
# pvcreate /dev/vdax
# vgcreate datastore /dev/vdax -s 16M
# lvcreate -l 50 -n database datastore
# mkfs.ext3 /dev/datastore/database
# mkdir /mnt/database
# mount /dev/datastore/database /mnt/database/
# df -Th
```

vi /etc/fstab
/dev/datastore /database /mnt/database/ ext3 defaults 0 0 mount -a

QUESTION 45

The /data directory is shared from the server1.example.com server.
When user tries to access, it should automatically mount.
When user doesn't use the mounted directory should unmount automatically after 50 seconds.
Shared directory should mount on /mnt/data.

Correct Answer/Explanation:
vi /etc/auto.master
/mnt /etc /auto.misc -timeout=50
vi /etc/auto.misc
data -rw,soft,intr server1.example.com:/data
service autofs restart
chkconfig autofs on
When you mount the other filesystem, you should unmount the mounted filesystem.
The automount feature of Linux helps to mount at access time and after certain seconds. When a user stops accessing the mounted directory, it automatically unmounts the filesystem.
/etc/auto.master is the master configuration file for autofs service. When you start the service, it reads the mount point as defined in the /etc/auto.master.

QUESTION 46

Make on data that only the user owner and group owner member can fully access.

Correct Answer/Explanation:
chmod 770 /data
ls -ld /data (Verify, it should look like the below output.)
drwxrwx-- 2 root sysadmin 4096 Mar 16 18:08 /data

To change the permission on the directory use chmod.
The directions want only the owner user (root) and group member (sysadmin) to fully access the directory: chmod 770 /data

QUESTION. 47

Some users' home directories are shared from your system. Using the showmount -e localhost command, the shared directory is not shown. Make the shared users' home directory accessible.

Correct Answer/Explanation:
cat /etc/exports (Verify whether the file is shared or not)
service nfs start (Start the NFS service)
service portmap start (Start the portmap service)
chkconfig nfs on (Automatically start the NFS service start automatically on next reboot)
chkconfig portmap on (Automatically start the portmap service on next reboot)
showmount -e localhost (Verify whether sharing or not)
• Check that default firewall is running on system.
• If default firewall is running, flush the iptables using iptables -F and stop the iptables service.

QUESTION 48

According the following requirements, configure autofs service and automatically mount to user's home directory in the LDAP domain.

• Instructor.example.com (192.168.0.254) has shared /home/guests/ldapuserX home directory to your system over an NFS export, where X is your hostname number.

• LdapuserX's home directory exists in instructor.example.com: /home/guests/ldapuserX

• LdapuserX's home directory must be able to automatically mount to /home/guests/ldapuserX on your system.

• Home directory must have write permissions for the corresponding user.

However, you can log on to the ldapuser1 - ldapuser99 users after verification. But you can only get your corresponding ldapuser users. If your system's hostname is server1.example.com, you can only get ldapuser1's home directory.

Correct Answer/Explanation:
mkdir -p /home/guests
cat /etc/auto.master
/home/guests /etc/auto.ldap
cat /etc/auto.ldap:
ldapuser1 -rw instructor.example.com:/home/guests/ldapuser1

automatically mount all the users home directory's:
* -rw instructor.example.com:/home/guests/&

QUESTION 49

Find all files or directories with sizes of 10k under the /etc directory, and copy to the /tmp/findfiles directory.
Find all the files or directories with Lucy as the owner, and copy to the /tmp/findfiles directory.

Correct Answer/Explanation:
find /etc -size 10k -exec cp {} /tmp/findfiles \;
find / -user lucy -exec cp -a {} /tmp/findfiles \;

If finding users and permissions, then use cp - a option, to keep file permissions and user attributes, etc.

QUESTION 50

Add 3 users: harry, natasha, tom.
Two users: harry, natasha are added to the admin additional (secondary) group.
Tom's login shell should be non-interactive.

Correct Answer/Explanation:
useradd -G admin harry
useradd -G admin natasha
useradd -s /sbin/nologin tom
id harry; id natasha (Shows secondary (supplemental) group membership)
cat /etc/passwd (Shows the login shell)
OR
system-config-users

QUESTION 51

Install dialogue package from an NFS share of a RHEL6 DVD.
The NFS share is found at instructor.example.com:/var/ftp/pub/rhel6/dvd

Correct Answer/Explanation:
yum http://instructor.example.comlpub/rhel6/dvd
ldap http//instructor.example.com pub/EXAMPLE-CA-CERT
yum install dialog (Install dialog package)

QUESTION 52

Your System is configured on the 192.168.0.0/24 network and your nameserver is 192.168.0.254. Make your system resolve to server1.example.com.

Correct Answer/Explanation:
The nameserver is specified in question and should be in resolv.conf.
vi /etc/resolv.conf
nameserver 192.168.0.254
host server1.example.com

QUESTION 53

Find out all the columns that contains the string seismic within /usr/share/dict/words, then copy all these columns to /root/lines.tx in original order, there is no blank line, and all columns must be an accurate copy of the original columns.

Correct Answer/Explanation:
grep seismic /usr/share/dict/words> /root/lines.txt

QUESTION 54

You have a domain named www.rhce.com with associated IP address 192.100.0.2. Configure the Apache web server by implementing SSL for encryption.

Correct Answer/Explanation:
vi /etc/httpd/conf.d/ssl.conf
<VirtualHost 192.100.0.2>
ServerName www.rhce.com
DocumentRoot /var/www/rhce
DirectoryIndex index.html index.htm
ServerAdmin webmaster@rhce.com
SSLEngine on
SSLCertificateFile /etc/httpd/conf/ssl.crt/server.crt
SSLCertificateKeyFile /etc/httpd/conf/ssl.key/server.key
</VirtualHost>
cd /etc/httpd/conf
make testcert
Create the directory and index page on specified path. (Index page can be downloaded from ftp:// server1.example.com at exam time)

service httpd start (or restart)

chkconfig httpd on

Apache can provide encrypted communications using SSL (Secure Socket Layer). To make use of encrypted communication, a client must request to https protocol, which is uses port 443. For HTTPS protocol to function, the certificate file and key file are both necessary.

QUESTION 55

Create a Shared Directory named /home/admins

/home/admins belongs to the group adminuser

This directory can be read and written to by members of group adminuser. Any files created in /home/ the adminuser group is automatically set.

Correct Answer/Explanation:

mkdir /home/admins

chgrp -R adminuser /home/admins

chmod g+w /home/admins

chmod g+s /home/admins

QUESTION 56

Create a user named alex, and the user id should be 1234, and the password should be alex111.

Correct Answer/Explanation:

useradd -u 1234 alex

passwd alex

alex111

alex111

OR

echo alex111 | passwd -stdin alex

QUESTION 57

Create a local directory named /common/admin.

• This directory is assigned to the admin group

• This directory has read, write and execute permissions for all admin group members.

• Other groups and users don't have any permissions.

• All the documents or directories created in /common/admin automatically inherit the admin group.

Correct Answer/Explanation:

mkdir -p /common/admin

chgrp admin /common/admin

chmod 2770 /common/admin

QUESTION 58

Add admin group and set gid=600

Correct Answer/Explanation:

groupadd -g 600 admin

QUESTION 59

Create swap space, set the size to 600MB, and make it mounted automatically after rebooting the system (a permanent mount).

Correct Answer/Explanation:
```
# dd if=/dev/zero of=/swapfile bs=1M count=600
# mkswap /swapfile
# vi /etc/fstab
/swapfile swap swap defaults 0 0 mount -a
```

QUESTION 60

Upgrading the kernel to 2.6.38.3.1, and configure the system to start the default kernel, keeping the old kernel available.

Correct Answer/Explanation:
```
# cat /etc/grub.conf
# cd /boot
# lftp it
# get dr/dom/kernel-xxxxx.rpm
# rpm -ivh kernel-xxxxx.rpm
# vim /etc/grub.conf
default=0
```

QUESTION 61

Configure a task: plan to run echo hello command at 14:23 every day.

ExplanationJReference:
```
# which echo
# crontab -e 23 14 /bin/echo hello
# crontab -l  (Verify configuration. )
```

QUESTION 62

Open kmcrl value of 5, & verify in /proc/cmdline

Correct Answer/Explanation:
```
# vim /boot/grub/grub.conf
kernel/vmlinuz-2.6.38-71.el6.x86_64 ro root=/dev/mapper/GLSvg-GLSrootrd_LVM_LV=GLSvg/GLSroot
rd_LVM_LV=GLSvg/GLSswaprd_NO_LUKSrd_NO_MDrd_NO_DM
LANG=en_US.UTF-8 SYSFONT=latarcyrheb-sun16 KEYBOARDTYPE=pc KEYTABLE=us crashkemel=auto
rhgb quiet kmcrl=5
Restart (to take effect) and verification:
# cat /proc/cmdline
ro root=/dev/mapper/GLSvg-GLSroot rd_LVM_LV=GLSvg/GLSroot rd_LVM_LV=GLSvg/GLSswap
rd_NO_LUKS rd_NO_MD rd_NO_DM
LANG=en_US.UTF-8 SYSFONT=latarcyrheb-sun16 KEYBOARDTYPE=pc KEYTABLE=us rhgb quiet
kmcrl=5
```

QUESTION 63

There are two networks, 192.168.00/24 and 192.168.1.0/24. Your system is in 192.168.0.0/24. One RHEL6 installed system will be used as a router. All required configuration is already done on the Linux server. 192.168.0.254 and 192.168.1.254 IP address are both assigned on that Linux server. How do you ping hosts on network 192.168.1.0/24?

Correct Answer/Explanation:

```
# vi/etc/sysconfig/network
GATEWAY=192.168.0.254
OR
# vi /etc/sysconf/network-scripts/ifdg-eth0
DEVICE=eth0
BOOTPROTO=static
ONBOOT=yes
IPADDR=192.168.0.?
NETMASK=255.255.255.0
GATEWAY=192.168.0.254
# service network restart
```

Gateway defines the way for packets to exit the network via a router. The Linux system is working as a router for two networks has both IP addresses: 192.168.0.254 and 192.168.1.254.

QUESTION 64

Create the following users, groups, and group memberships. A group named adminuser.
A user natasha who belongs to adminuser as a secondary (supplemental) group.
A user harry who also belongs to adminuser as a secondary (supplemental) group.
A user sarah who does not have access to an interactive shell on the system, and who is not a member of adminuser. Natasha, harry, and sarah should all have the password set to redhat.

Correct Answer/Explanation:

```
# groupadd adminuser
# useradd -G adminuser natasha
# useradd -G adminuser harry
# useradd -s /sbin/nologin sarah
# passwd natasha
# passwd harry
# passwd sarah
```

QUESTION 65

Install the appropriate kernel update from http://server.domain11.example.com/pub/updates. The updated kernel must be the default kernel when the system is rebooted.
The original kernel remains available and bootable on the system.

Correct Answer/Explanation:

```
# ftp server.domain11.example.com Anonymous login
ftp> cd /pub/updates
ftp> ls
ftp> mget kernel*
ftp> bye
```

```
# rpm -ivh kernel*
# vim /etc/grub.conf
set default=0
```
The set default=0 verifies that the updated kernel is the first kernel and the original kernel remains available.
wq!

QUESTION 66
Update the kernel from ftp://instructor.example.com/pub/updates with the following requirements:
- The updated kernel must exist as default kernel after rebooting the system.
- The original kernel still exists and is available in the system.

Correct Answer/Explanation:
```
# rpm -ivh kernel-firm...
# rpm -ivh kernel...
```

QUESTION 67
A yum source has been provided at http://instructor.example.com/pub/rhel6/dvd
Configure your system using that yum source.

Correct Answer/Explanation:
```
# vi /etc/yum.repos.d/base.repo
[base]
name=base
baseurl=http://instructor.example.com/pub/rhel6/dvd
gpgcheck=O
yum list
```

QUESTION 68
Configure a task/plan to run the command echo "file" at 14:23 every day.

Correct Answer/Explanation:
- Created as administrator
```
# crontab -u natasha -e 23 14 * * * /bin/echo "file"
```
- Created as natasha
```
# su - natasha
# crontab -e 23 14 * * * /bin/echo "file"
```

QUESTION 69
You are new System Administrator and from now you are going to handle the system and your main task is network monitoring, backup and restore. But you don't know the root password. Change the root password to "redhat" and login using the default runlevel.

Correct Answer/Explanation:
When you boot the system, it starts on the runlevel specified in /etc/inittab:
id:?:initdefault:

To change the root password you need to boot the system into single user mode and modify the boot loader command to append "rd.break"
- Interrupt the boot loader countdown by pressing a key.
- Select the entry that needs to be booted.
- Press e to edit that entry.
- Move the cursor to the command line containing the kernel, which is line that starts with linux16, and append rd.break

This will break the initialization process just before control is handed from the initramfs to the Linux system kernel with a new systemd instance. The initramfs prompt will show up on whatever type of shell prompt is specified last on that kernel command line. You will need to press Ctrl+X to boot with these changes.
Now a root shell will be shown, with the root file system for the actual system mounted on /sysroot as read-only.
- Remount /sysroot as read-write.
        switch_root:/# mount -oremount,rw /sysroot
- Switch into a chroot jail, this is where /sysroot is treated as the root of the file system tree.
        switch_root:/# chroot /sysroot
- Set a new root password:
        bash# passwd root
- If you have SELinux enabled, ensure all unlabeled files (including /etc/shadow) get relabeled during boot:
        bash# touch /.autorelabel
- Type exit twice. This will first exit the chroot jail, and the second one will exit the initramfs debug shell.

QUESTION 70
Configure autofs to automount the home directories of LDAP users as follows:
hostdomain11.example_com NFS-exports /home to your system.
This filesystem contains a pre-configured home directory for the user ldapuser11.
ldapuser11's home directory is hostdomain11.example.com /rhome/ldapuser11 ldapuser11's home directory should be automounted locally beneath /rhome as /rhome/ldapuser11
Home directories must be writable by their users.
ldapuser11's password is "password"

Correct Answer/Explanation:
\# vim /etc/auto.master
/rhome /etc/auto.misc
\# vim /etc/auto.misc
ldapuser11 --rw,sync host.domain11.example.com:/rhome/ldpauser11
\# service autofs restart
\# service autofs reload
\# chkconfig autofs on
\# su -ldapuser11
Login ldapuser with home directory
\# exit

QUESTION 71
Mount the iso image /root/examine.iso to /mnt/iso, and then enable automatic mount (permanent mount).

Correct Answer/Explanation:
```
# mkdir -p /mnt/iso
# vi /etc/fstab
/root/examine.iso /mnt/iso iso9660 loop 0 0 mount -a
# mount I grep examine
```

QUESTION 72
Create a volume group, vg1, and set 16M as a extend size and containing 50 extends on logical volume lv02, make it an ext4 file system, and mounted automatically under /mnt/data.

Correct Answer/Explanation:
```
# pvcreate /dev/sda7 /dev/sda8
# vgcreate -s 16M vg1 /dev/sda7 /dev/sda8
# lvcreate -l 50 -n lvm02
# mkfs.ext4 /dev/vg1/lvm02
# blkid /dev/vg1/lv1
Copy UUID=XXXXX
# vim /etc/fstab
UUID=xxxxxxxx /mnt/data ext4 defaults 0 0
# mkdir -p /mnt/data
# mount -a
# mount
```

QUESTION 73
Create a 2G swap partition which take effect automatically at boot, and it should not affect the original swap partition.

Correct Answer/Explanation:
```
# fdisk /dev/sda
p        ( checks partitions table )
n        ( for new partition)
I        ( for logical partition)
Enter    ( for the starting cylinder)
+2G      ( for the final cylinder)
t        ( to change the System ID of partition )
82       ( 82 means Linux Swap )
p        ( p to verify the partitions lists and remember the partition's name for below )
w        ( to write on partitions table )
# partx -a /dev/sda
# partprobe ( or reboot )
# mkswap /dev/sda8
Copy UUID=XXXXX
# swapon -a
# vim /etc/fstab
```

UUID=XXXXX swap swap defaults 0 0
# swapon -s

QUESTION 74
Set file permissions on /archive directory so that only the user owner and group owner can fully access.

Correct Answer/Explanation:
chmod 770 /archive
ls -ld /archive verify , so preview should look like:
drwxrwx--- 2 root sysuser 4096 Mar 16 17:01 /archive
To change the permission on directory, use the chmod command. The question requires that only
the owner user (root) and group member (sysuser) can fully access the directory so the correct chmod
command is:
chmod 770 /archive

QUESTION 75
Configure a user account with user name iar and uid 3400. Password is redhat

Correct Answer/Explanation:
useradd -u 3400 iar
passwd iar

QUESTION 76
Locate all the files owned by ira and copy them to the /root/findresults directory.

Correct Answer/Explanation:
find / -user ira > /root/findresults (If /root/findfiles is a file.)
mkdir -p /root/findresults
find / -user ira -exec cp -a {} /root/findresults \; (If /root/findfiles is a directory.)
ls /root/findresults

QUESTION 77
Create a backup file named /root/backup.tar.bz2, contains the content of /usr/local. The tar must use
bzip2 compression.

Correct Answer/Explanation:
cd /usr/local
tar -jcvf /root/backup.tar.bz2
mkdir /test
tar -jxvf /root/backup.tar.bz2 -C /test (Decompression to check the content is the same as the
/usr/local
If the questions require using gzip to compress, then change -j to -z.

QUESTION 78
Install kernel update from: http://lserver.domain11.example.com/pub/updates.

The updated kernel must be used as the default kernel of the system start-up.
The original kernel is still valid and can be selected when the Linux system starts up.

Correct Answer/Explanation:
Using the browser open the URL in the question, download kernel file to root or home directory.
uname -r (Check the current kernelversion.)
rpm -ivh kernel-*.rpm
vi /boot/grub.conf (Verify GRUB configuration)
Some questions are: Install and upgrade the kernel as required and ensure that grub2 is the default item for startup. The yum repo should be set to http://content.example.com/rhel7.0/x86-64/errata
OR
uname -r (Check kernel version.)
yum-config-manager --add-repo=http://content.example.com/rhel7.0/x86-64/errata
yum clean all
yum list kernel
yum -y install kernel
Default enable new kernel grub2-editenv list
Modify grub2-set-default "kernel full name"
grub2-mkconfig -o /boot/grub2/grub.cfg

QUESTION 79
Add an extra 500M swap partition to your system. The swap partition should mount automatically when the system starts up. Don't remove and/or modify the existing swap partitions on your system.

Correct Answer/Explanation:
fdisk -cu /dev/vda
partx -a /dev/vda
mkswap /dev/vdax
swapon /dev/vdax
swapon -s
vi /etc/fstab
/dev/vdax swap swap defaults 0 0
mount -a

QUESTION 80
Configure the NTP service in your system.

Correct Answer/Explanation:
system-config-date &

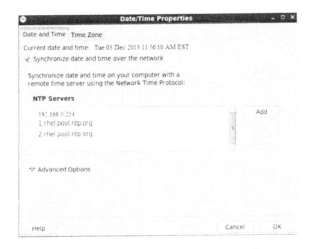

QUESTION 81
Who ever creates the files/directories on archive group owner should automatically be the same group owner of the archive.

Correct Answer/Explanation:
chmod g+s /archrve
ls -ld /archive
drwxrws--- 2 root sysuser 4096 Jan 01 17:01 /archive
If SGID bit is set on the directory then every user that creates the files in the directory has group owner set to the owner of parent directory.
To set the SGID bit:
chmod g+s directory
To remove the SGID bit:
chmod g-s directory

QUESTION 82
Download ftp://192.168.0.254/pub/boot.iso to /root, and mount it automatically under /media/cdrom and make it take effect automatically at boot.

Correct Answer/Explanation:
cd /root
wget ftp://192.168.0.254/pub/boot.iso
mkdir -p /media/cdrom
vim /etc/fstab
/root/boot.iso /media/cdrom iso9660 defaults,loop 0 0
mount -a   (mount syntax: mount [-t vfstype] [-o options] device_dir)

QUESTION 83
Add a new logical partition having a 100MB size, and create the data which will be the mount point for the new partition.

Correct Answer/Explanation:
fdisk /dev/hda
n   (for new partition)

```
l          ( for logical partitions )
Enter    ( for starting Cylinder)
+100M  ( for finishing Cylinder)
p          ( p to verify the partitions lists and remember the partition's name for below )
w          ( to write on partitions table )
# partprobe  ( or reboot )
# mkfs -t ext3 /dev/hda6
OR
# mke2fs -j /dev/hda6 ( create ext3 filesystem )
# vi /etc/fstab
/dev/hda6 /data ext3 defaults 0 0
# mount  /dev/hda6 /data ( verify by mounting)
```

QUESTION 84

Create a volume group, and set the size to 500M, the size of single PE is 16M. Create logical volume named lv0 in this volume group, set size is 20 PE, make it an ext3 file system, and make it mounted automatically under data.

Correct Answer/Explanation:
```
# fdisk /dev/vda
# pvcreate /dev/vda3
# vgcreate -s 16M vg0 /dev/vda3
# lvcreate -n lv0 -l 20 vg0
# mkfs.ext3 /dev/mapper/vg0-lv0
# mkdir /data
# vi /etc/fstab
/dev/mapper/vg0-lv0 /data ext3 defaults 0 0
# mount -a
# mount | grep data
```

QUESTION 85

The firewall must be open.

Correct Answer/Explanation:
```
# /etc/init.d/iptables start
# iptables -F
# iptables -X
# iptables -Z
# /etc/init.d/iptables save
# chkconfig iptables on
```

QUESTION 86

The system ldap.example.com provides an LDAP authentication service. Your system should bind to this service as follows:
The base DN for the authentication service is dc=domain11, dc=example, dc=com.
LDAP is used to provide both account information and authentication information. The connection must be encrypted using the certificate at http://host.domain11.example.com/pub/domain11.crt

When properly configured, ldapuserX should be able to log into your system, but will not have a home directory until you have completed the autofs requirement. Username: ldapuser11, Password: password

Correct Answer/Explanation:
# system-config-authentication LDAP user DN=dc=domain11,dc=example,dc=com
server=hostdomain11.example.com
certificate=
http://host.domain11.example.com/pub/domain11.crt LDAP password
OK
starting sssd
su - ldapuser11 (Verify Bash prompt is displayed)
exit

QUESTION 87
Create a catalog under /home named admins. Its respective group is requested to be the admin group. The group users should be able to read and write, while other users are not allowed to access it. The files created by users from the same group should also be the admin group.

Correct Answer/Explanation:
cd /home/
mkdir admins/
chown admin admins/
chmod 770 admins/
chmod g+s admins/

QUESTION 88
Create one partition having size 100MB and mount it on data.

Correct Answer/Explanation:
fdisk dev/had
n   (for new partitions)
l   (press l for logical)
Enter   (for the starting cylinder)
+100M (for the final cylinder)
p   (p to verify the partitions lists. Remember the partition's name to be used below)
w   (to write on partitions table.)
partprobe (or reboot)
mkfs -t ext3 /dev/hda7
OR
mke2fs -j /dev/hda7
vi /etc/fstab
/dev/hda7 /data ext3 defaults 1 2
mount /dev/hda7 /data

QUESTION 89

Resize the logical volume vo and its filesystem to 290 MB. Make sure that the filesystem contents remain intact. Partitions are seldom exactly the same size as requested, so a size within the range of 260 MB to 320 MB is acceptable.

Correct Answer/Explanation:
df -hT
lvextend -L +100M /dev/vg0/vo
lvscan
xfs_growfs /home/ (/home is LVM mounted directory)
Note: This step is only needed in our practice environment, you do not need to do it in the real exam
resize2fs /dev/vg0/vo (Use this command to update in the real exam)
df -hT
OR
e2fsck -f /dev/vg0/vo
umount /home
resize2fs /dev/vg0/vo
lvreduce -l 100M /dev/vg0/vo
mount /dev/vg0/vo /home
df -Ht

QUESTION 90

Configure the permissions of /var/tmp/fstab
Copy the file /etc/fstab to /var/tmp/fstab. Configure the permissions of /var/tmp/fstab so that:
The file /var/tmp/fstab is owned by the root user.
The file /var/tmp/fstab belongs to the group root.
The file /var/tmp/fstab should not be executable by anyone.
The user natasha is able to read and write /var/tmp/fstab.
The user harry can neither write nor read /var/tmp/fstab.
All other users (including current & future) have the ability to read /var/tmp/fstab.

Correct Answer/Explanation:
cp -a /etc/fstab /var/tmp
cd /var/tmp
ls -l
getfacl /var/tmp/fstab
chmod ugo-x /var/tmp/fstab (No need to do this, there won't be execute permission for the file by default)
setfacl -m u:natasha:rw /var/tmp/fstab
setfacl -m u:harry:0 /var/tmp/fstab (Read permission will be there for all the users, by default.)
ls -l /var/tmp/fstab (Verify)
ls -la /var/tmp/fstab (Verify)

QUESTION 91

Copy /etc/fstab file to /var/tmp directory. The fstab file in /var/tmp must have the following set.
• The owner of fstab must be root.
• fstab belongs to the root group.
• User mary have read and write permissions for fstab.

- User alice have read and execute permissions for fstab.
- Create a user bob, set uid is 1000. Bob must have read and write permissions for fstab.
- All users have read permission for fstab.

Correct Answer/Explanation:
cp /etc/fstab /var/tmp
chown root:root /var/tmp/fstab
chmod a-x /var/tmp/fstab
setfacl -m u:mary:rw /var/tmp/fstab
setfacl -m u:alice:rx /var/tmp/fstab
useradd -u 1000 bob

QUESTION 92
Search files.
Find out files owned by jack, and copy them to directory /root/findresults

Correct Answer/Explanation:
mkdir /rootlfindfiles
find / -user jack -exec cp -a {} /root/findfiles/ \; ls /root/findresults

QUESTION 93
There is a local logical volume in your system, belong to vgsrv volume group, mounted to the /common directory. The size is 128MB.
Extend the logical volume to 190 MB without any loss of data. The size allowed is between 160-190 MB after extending.

Correct Answer/Explanation:
lvextend -L 190M /dev/mapper/vgsrv-common resize2fs /dev/mapper/vgsrv-common

QUESTION 94
One logical volume named /dev/test0/testvolume1 is created. The initial size of that disk is 100MB, extend it 200MB more while online without reboot.

Correct Answer/Explanation:
lvextend -L +200M /dev/test0/testvolume1 (Use lvdisplay /dev/test0/testvolume1 to verify)
ext2online -d /dev/test0/testvolume1

The lvextend command is used to increase the size of Logical Volume.
The other command lvresize command can also be used. To bring the increased size on online we used the ext2online command.

QUESTION 95
Make a swap partition with 100MB. Make it automatically usable at boot.

Correct Answer/Explanation:
fdisk /dev/hda
n   (for new partition)
l   (for logical partition)

Enter (for the starting cylinder)
+100M (for the final cylinder)
p   (p to verify the partitions lists and remember the partition's name for below)
t   (to change the System ID of partition)
82   (82 means Linux Swap)
w   (to write on partitions table)
partprobe (or reboot)
mkswap /dev/hda? (create swap file system on partition)
swapon /dev/hda? (enable the swap space)
free -m (verify either swap is enabled or not)
vi /etc/fstab
/dev/hda? swap swap defaults 0 0
Reboot the and verify that swap is automatically enabled.

QUESTION 96

One logical volume named lv1 is created under vg0. The Initial Size of that logical volume is 100MB. Resize that logical volume to 500M without losing any data. It should be increased online without reboot.

Correct Answer/Explanation:

The LVM system organizes hard disks into Logical Volume (LV) groups. Physical hard disk partitions (or possibly RAID arrays) are set up in a bunch of equal sized chunks known as PhysicalExtents (PE).

Physical Volume (PV) is the standard partition that you add to the LVM.
Normally a physical volume is a standard primary or logical partition, but it can also be a RAID array. PhysicalExtent (PE) is a chunk of disk space. Every PV is divided into a number of equal sized PEs. Every PE in a LV group is the same size. Different LV groups can have different sized PEs. Logical Extent (LE) is also a chunk of disk space. Every LE gets mapped to a specific PE by an administrator.
Logical Volume (LV) is composed of a group of LEs from a Volume Group (VG). You can mount a file system such as /home and /var on an LV.
A Logical Volumes (LV) is composed of a Volume Group (VG). Most of the commands that are available apply to a specific Volume Group (VG).

lvdisplay /dev/vg0/lv1 (Verify the size of logical volume lv1)
df -h or df -h (Verify the size on mounted directory)
lvextend -L +400M /dev/vg0/lv1
ext2online -d /dev/vg0/lv1 (bring extended size online immediately)
lvdisplay (Verify)
df -h (Verify)

QUESTION 97

One logical volume named as myvol is created from the vo volume group and is mounted. The initial size of that logical volume is 400MB. Reduce the size of the logical volume to 200MB without losing any data. The size of logical volume from 200MB to 210MB will be acceptable.

Correct Answer/Explanation:

lvdisplay /dev/vo/myvol (Check the size)
fsck -f /dev/vo/myvol (Make sure that the filesystem is in a consistent state before reducing.)
resize2fs /dev/vo/myvol 200M (Reduce the filesystem by 200MB.)
lvreduce /dev/vo/myvol -L 200M (It is now possible to reduce the logical volume.)
lvdisplay /dev/vo/myvol (Verify)
df -h (Verify new size is online)

QUESTION 98
Create a collaborative directory /home/admins.
Group ownership /home/admins is adminuser.
The directory should be readable, writable, and accessible to members of adminuser, but not to any other users, except root.
Files created in /home/admins automatically have group ownership set to the adminuser group.

Correct Answer/Explanation:
mkdir /home/admins
chgrp -R adminuser /home/admins
chmod g+w /home/admins
chmod g+s /home/admins

QUESTION 99
There is a logical volume named shrink and belonging to the vgsrv volume group, & mounted to the /shrink directory. The size is 320MB. Reduce the logical volume to 220MB without any loss of data. The size is allowed between 200MB - 260MB.

Correct Answer/Explanation:
cd
umount /shrink
e2fsck -f /dev/mapper/vgsrv-shrink
resize2fs /dev/mapper/vgsrv-shrink 220M
lvreduce -L 220M /dev/mapper/vgsrv-shrink
mount -a

QUESTION 100
Upgrade the kernel, start the new kernel by default. Download kernel from this address:
ftp://server1.domain10.example.com/pub/update/new.kernel

Correct Answer/Explanation:
Download the new kernel file and then install it
[root@desktop2 Desktop]# ls
kernel-2.6.38-71.7.1.el6.x86_64.rpm
kernel-firmware-2.6.38-71.7.1.el6.noarch.rpm
[root@desktop2 Desktop]# rpm -ivh kernel-*
Preparing... ####################################
[100%]
1:kernel-firmware
################################### [50 %]
2:kernel

```
######################################## [ 100 %]
```
Verify the grub.conf file, whether use the new kernel as the default boot.
```
[root@desktop8 Desktop]# cat /boot/grub/grub.conf
default=0
title Red Hat Enterpnse Linux Server (2.6.38-71.7.1.el6.x86_64)
root (hd0,0)
kernel /vmlinuz-2.6.38-71.7.1.el6.x86_64 ro root=/dev/mapper/vol0-root rd_LVM_LV=vol0/root
rd_NO_LUKS rd_NO_MD
rd_NO_DM LANG=en_US.UTF-8 SYSFONT=latarcyrheb-sun16 KEYBOARDTYPE=pc KEYTABLE=us
crashkernel=auto rhgb quiet
initrd /initramfs-2.6.38-71.7.1.ef6.x86_64.img
```

QUESTION 101
Add user: user1, set uid to 601 with password set to "redhat"
The user's login shell should be non-interactive.

Correct Answer/Explanation:
```
# useradd -u 601 -s /sbin/nologin user1
# passwd user1
redhat
```

QUESTION 102
Setup your Linux system as a router for 172.24.0.0/16 and 172.25.0.0/16. Enable IP Forwarding.
```
# echo "1" >/proc/sys/net/ipv4/ip_forward
# vi /etc/sysctl.conf net.ipv4.ip_forward=1
```

Correct Answer/Explanation:
/proc is the virtual filesystem, containing the information about the running kernel.
To change a parameter of a running kernel you should modify /proc. Kernel will take the value from /etc/sysctl.conf on next boot.

QUESTION 103
Add users: user2, user3.
The secondary (supplemental) group of the two users is the admin group. Set both passwords to "redhat".

Correct Answer/Explanation:
```
# useradd -G admin user2
# useradd -G admin user3
# passwd user2
redhat
# passwd user3
redhat
```

QUESTION 104
Configure your system so that it is an NTP client of server.domain11.example.com

Correct Answer/Explanation:

system-config-date
Check mark "Synchronize date and time over network."
Remove all the NTP SERVER and click ADD and type server.domain11.example.com

QUESTION 105
There is a server having 2 ip addresses assigned, 172.24.254.254, and 172.25.254.254. Your system lies on the 172.24.0.0/16 subnet. Ping to 172.25.254.254 by assigning the following IP: 172.24.0.1.

Correct Answer/Explanation:
netconfig (Use netconfig command)
Enter the IP address as 172.24.0.1
Enter Subnet Mask
Enter Default Gateway and primary name server
Enter ok
ifdown eth0
ifup eth0
ifconfig (Verify)
In the lab, the server is already playing the role of router (IP forwarding is enabled).
Just set the correct IP and gateway, and then it is possible to ping to 172.25.254.254.

QUESTION 106
Set SELinux in enforcing mode.

Correct Answer/Explanation:
# getenforce (Checks the current mode of SELinux)
# getenforce 1 (Runs SELinux in enforcing mode)
# getenforce (Checks the current mode of SELinux)
# vim /etc/selinux/config   (Modify config to make changes take effect at boot)
selinux=enforcing
# sestatus (Verify)

QUESTION 107
Copy /etc/fstab to /var/tmp. Change fstab's group name in /var/tmp to admin. The user1 should be able to read, write, & modify it, while user2 has no permissions.

Correct Answer/Explanation:
cp /etc/fstab /var/tmp/
chgrp admin /var/tmp/fstab
setfacl -m u:user1:rwx /var/tmp/fstab
setfacl -m u:user2:--- /var/tmp/fstab
ls -l
-rw-rw-r--+ 1 root admin 685 Dec 1 11:01 /var/tmp/fstab

QUESTION 108
Binding to an external validation server.
System server.domain11.example.com provides an LDAP validation service. Your system should bind to this service as required:
Base DN of validation service is dc=example,dc=com

LDAP is used for providing account information and validation information. Connecting using the certificate at http://server.domain11.example.com/pub/EXAMPLE-CA-CERT.
After the configuration, ldapuser1 can log into your system, it does not have a home directory until you finish autofs questions. ldapuser1 password is "password".

Correct Answer/Explanation:
yum -y install sssd authconfig-gtk krb5-workstation authconfig-gtk
Open the graphical interface
Modify user account database to ldap.
Complete DN and LDAP SERVER.
Check box to use TLS to encrypt connections.
Use http://server.domain11.example.com/pub/EXAMPLE-CA-CERT to download ca
Authentication method: choose LDAP password
Id ldapuser1 (Verify ldapuser1 is added)

QUESTION 109
Create the following user, group and group membership: adminuser group
User natasha, using adminuser as a secondary (supplemental) group.
User harry, also using adminuser as a secondary (supplemental) group.
User sarah, should not access the shell which is interactive in the system, and is not a member of adminuser. All passwords are "redhat".

Correct Answer/Explanation:
groupadd adminuser
useradd natasha -G adminuser
useradd harry -G adminuser
useradd sarah -s /sbin/nologin
passwd username (to modify password)
OR
echo redhat | passwd -stdin username
id natasha (Verify user group membership)

QUESTION 110
Create a user alex with a userid of 3400. The password for this user should be "redhat".

Correct Answer/Explanation:
useradd -u 3400 alex
passwd alex
su - alex (Verify)

QUESTION 111
One domain Red Hat Enterprise Linux server is configured in your lab. Your domain server is server1.example.com. nisuser2001, nisuser2002, nisuser2003 are created on your server with IP address and home directory set to 192.168.0.254:rhome/stationx/nisuser2001. Make sure that when a nisuser logs into your system, it automatically mounts the home directory. Home directory is separately shared on server /rhome/stationx/ where x is your station number.

Correct Answer/Explanation:

Use authconfig --nisserver=<NIS SERVER> --nisdomain=<NIS DOMAIN> --update

Example:

authconfig --nisserver=192.168.0.254 --nisdomain=RHCE --update or system-config- authentication

Click on Enable NIS

Type the NIS Domain: RHCE

Type Server 192.168.0.254 then click on next and ok, and ok.

Create a directory /rhome/stationx where x is your station number.

vi /etc/auto.master

/rhome/stationx /etc/auto.home --timeout=60

vi /etc/auto.home

* -rw,soft,intr 192.168.0.254:/rhome/stationx/&

Specify your station number in the place of x.

service autofs restart

Login as the nisuser2001 or nisuser2002 from another terminal should be successful. According to question, RHCE domain is already configured. We have to make a client of RHCE domain and automatically mount the home directory on your system. To make a member of domain, we use the authconfig with options or system-config-authentication command. There are lots of authentication server types, such as NIS, LDAP, SMB. NIS is a RPC related service, so there's no need to configure the DNS server, we only have to specify the NIS server address.

The automount feature is available. When a user tries to login, the home directory will automatically mount. The automount service used the /etc/auto.master file. In the /etc/auto.master file we specified the mount point & the configuration file for the mount point.